THE GRAND INQUISITOR

Fyodor Dostoyevsky Biography

Fyodor Mikhailovich Dostoyevsky (11 November 1821 – 9 February 1881), sometimes transliterated Dostoevsky, was a Russian novelist, short story writer, essayist, journalist and philosopher. Dostoyevsky's literary works explore human psychology in the troubled political, social, and spiritual atmosphere of 19th-century Russia. Many of his works are marked by a preoccupation with Christianity, explored through the prism of the individual confronted with life's hardships and beauty.

He began writing in his 20s, and his first novel, Poor Folk, was published in 1846 when he was 25. His major works include Crime and Punishment (1866), The Idiot (1869), Demons (1872) and The Brothers Karamazov (1880). His output consists of 11 novels, three novellas, 17 short novels and numerous other works. Many literary critics rate him as one of the greatest psychologists in world literature. His 1864 novella Notes from Underground is considered to be one of the first works of existentialist literature.

Born in Moscow in 1821, Dostoyevsky was introduced to literature at an early age through fairy tales and legends, and through books by Russian and foreign authors. His mother died in 1837, when he was 15, and around the same time he left school to enter the Nikolayev Military Engineering Institute. After graduating, he worked as an engineer and briefly enjoyed a lavish lifestyle, translating books to earn extra money. In the mid-1840s he wrote his first novel, Poor Folk, which gained him entry into St. Petersburg's literary circles.

In 1849 he was arrested for his involvement in the Petrashevsky Circle, a secret society of liberal utopians that also functioned as a literary discussion group; they were particularly interested in the works of Charles Fourier. He and other members were condemned to death, but at the last moment, a note from Tsar Nicholas I was delivered to the scene of the firing squad, commuting the sentence to ten years' hard labour in Siberia. His seizures, which may have started in 1839, increased in frequency there, and he was diagnosed with epilepsy. On his release, he was forced to serve as a soldier, before being discharged on grounds of ill health.

In the following years, Dostoyevsky worked as a journalist, publishing and editing several magazines of his own and later A Writer's Diary, a collection of his writings. He began to travel around western Europe and developed a gambling addiction, which led to financial hardship. For a time, he had to beg for money, but he eventually became one of the most widely read and highly regarded Russian writers. His books have been translated into more than 170 languages. Dostoyevsky influenced a multitude of writers and philosophers, from Anton Chekhov and Ernest Hemingway to Friedrich Nietzsche and Jean-Paul Sartre.

Ancestry

Dostoyevsky's parents were part of a multi-ethnic and multi-denominational Ruthenian-Litvin noble family from the Pinsk region, with roots dating to the 16th century. Branches of the family included Russian Orthodox Christians, Roman Catholics and Eastern Catholics. Dostoyevsky's immediate ancestors on his mother's side were merchants; the male line on his father's side were priests. His father, Mikhail, was expected to join the clergy but instead ran away from home and broke with the family permanently.

In 1809 the 20-year-old Mikhail Dostoyevsky enrolled in Moscow's Imperial Medical-Surgical Academy. From there he was assigned to a Moscow hospital, where he served as military doctor, and in 1818 he was appointed senior physician. In 1819 he married Maria Nechayeva. The following year, he took up a post at the Mariinsky Hospital for the poor. After the birth of his first two sons, Mikhail and Fyodor, he was promoted to collegiate assessor, a position which raised his legal status to that of the nobility and enabled him to acquire a small estate in Darovoye, a town about 150 km (100 miles) from Moscow, where the family usually spent the summers. Dostoyevsky's parents subsequently had six more children: Varvara (1822–92), Andrei (1825–97), Lyubov (born and died 1829), Vera (1829–96), Nikolai (1831–83) and Aleksandra (1835–89).

Childhood (1821–1835)

Fyodor Dostoyevsky, born on 11 November [O.S. 30 October] 1821, the second child of Dr. Mikhail Dostoyevsky and Maria Dostoyevskaya (née Nechayeva). He was raised in the family home in the grounds of the Mariinsky Hospital for the Poor, which was in a lower class district on the edges of Moscow. Dostoyevsky encountered the patients, who were at the lower end of the Russian social scale, when playing in the hospital gardens.

Dostoyevsky was introduced to literature at an early age. From the age of three, he was read heroic sagas, fairy tales and legends by his nanny, Alena Frolovna, an especially influential figure in his childhood. When he was four his mother used the Bible to teach him to read and write. His parents introduced him to a wide range of literature, including Russian writers Karamzin, Pushkin and Derzhavin; Gothic fiction such as Ann Radcliffe; romantic works by Schiller and Goethe; heroic tales by Cervantes and Walter Scott; and Homer's epics. Although his father's approach to education has been described as strict and harsh, Dostoyevsky himself reports that his imagination was brought alive by nightly readings by his parents.

Some of his childhood experiences found their way into his writings. When a nine-year-old girl had been raped by a drunk, he was asked to fetch his father to attend to her. The incident haunted him, and the theme of the desire of a mature man for a young girl appears in The Devils, The Brothers Karamazov, and other writings. An incident involving a family servant, or serf, in the estate in Darovoye, is described in "The Peasant Marey": when the young Dostoyevsky imagines hearing a wolf in the forest, Marey, who is working nearby, comforts him.

Although Dostoyevsky had a delicate physical constitution, his parents described him as hot-headed, stubborn and cheeky. In 1833, Dostoyevsky's father, who was profoundly religious, sent him to a French boarding school and then to the Chermak boarding school. He was described as a pale, introverted dreamer and an over-excitable romantic. To pay the school fees, his father borrowed money and extended his private medical practice. Dostoyevsky felt out of place among his aristocratic classmates at the Moscow school, and the experience was later reflected in some of his works, notably The Adolescent.

Youth (1836–1843)

On 27 September 1837 Dostoyevsky's mother died of tuberculosis. The previous May, his parents had sent Dostoyevsky and his brother Mikhail to St Petersburg to attend the free Nikolayev Military Engineering Institute, forcing the brothers to abandon their academic studies for military careers. Dostoyevsky entered the academy in January 1838, but only with the help of family members. Mikhail was refused admission on health grounds and was sent to the Academy in Reval, Estonia. Dostoyevsky disliked the academy, primarily because of his lack of interest in science, mathematics and military engineering and his preference for drawing and architecture. As his friend Konstantin Trutovsky once said, "There was no student in the entire institution with less of a military bearing than F. M. Dostoyevsky. He moved clumsily and jerkily; his uniform hung awkwardly on him; and his knapsack, shako and rifle all looked like some sort of fetter he had been forced to wear for a time and which lay heavily on him." Dostoyevsky's character and interests made him an outsider among his 120 classmates: he showed bravery and a strong sense of justice, protected newcomers, aligned himself with teachers, criticised corruption among officers and helped poor farmers. Although he was solitary and inhabited his own literary world, he was respected by his classmates. His reclusiveness and interest in religion earned him the nickname "Monk Photius".

Signs of Dostoyevsky's epilepsy may have first appeared on learning of the death of his father on 16 June 1839, although the reports of a seizure originated from accounts written by his daughter (later expanded by Sigmund Freud.) which are now considered to be unreliable. His father's official cause of death was an apoplectic stroke, but a neighbour, Pavel Khotiaintsev, accused the father's serfs of murder. Had the serfs been found guilty and sent to Siberia, Khotiaintsev would have been in a position to buy the vacated land. The serfs were acquitted in a trial in Tula, but Dostoyevsky's brother Andrei perpetuated the story. After his father's death, Dostoyevsky continued his studies, passed his exams and obtained the rank of engineer cadet, entitling him to live away from the academy. He visited Mikhail in Reval, and frequently attended concerts, operas, plays and ballets. During this time, two of his friends introduced him to gambling.

On 12 August 1843 Dostoyevsky took a job as a lieutenant engineer and lived with Adolph Totleben in an apartment owned by Dr. Rizenkampf, a friend of Mikhail. Rizenkampf characterised him as "no less good-natured and no less courteous than his brother, but when not in a good mood he often looked at everything through dark glasses, became vexed, forgot good manners, and sometimes was carried away to the point of abusiveness and loss of self-awareness". Dostoyevsky's first completed literary work, a translation of Honoré de Balzac's novel Eugénie Grandet, was published in June and July 1843 in the 6th and 7th volume of the journal Repertoire and Pantheon, followed by several other translations. None were successful, and his financial difficulties led him to write a novel.

Early Career (1844–1849)

Dostoyevsky completed his first novel, Poor Folk, in May 1845. His friend Dmitry Grigorovich, with whom he was sharing an apartment at the time, took the manuscript to the poet Nikolay Nekrasov, who in turn showed it to the renowned and influential literary critic Vissarion Belinsky. Belinsky described it as Russia's first "social novel". Poor Folk was released on 15 January 1846 in the St Petersburg Collection almanac and became a commercial success.

Dostoyevsky felt that his military career would endanger his now flourishing literary career, so he wrote a letter asking to resign his post. Shortly thereafter, he wrote his second novel, The Double, which appeared in the journal Notes of the Fatherland on 30 January 1846, before being published in February. Around the same time, Dostoyevsky discovered socialism through the writings of French thinkers Fourier, Cabet, Proudhon and Saint-Simon. Through his relationship with Belinsky he expanded his knowledge of the philosophy of socialism. He was attracted to its logic, its sense of justice and its preoccupation with the destitute and the disadvantaged. However, his relationship with Belinsky became increasingly strained as Belinsky's atheism and dislike of religion clashed with Dostoyevsky's Russian Orthodox beliefs. Dostoyevsky eventually parted with him and his associates.

After The Double received negative reviews, Dostoyevsky's health declined and he had more frequent seizures, but he continued writing. From 1846 to 1848 he released several short stories in the magazine Annals of the Fatherland, including "Mr. Prokharchin", "The Landlady", "A Weak Heart", and "White Nights". These stories were unsuccessful, leaving Dostoyevsky once more in financial trouble, so he joined the utopian socialist Betekov circle, a tightly knit community which helped him to survive. When the circle dissolved, Dostoyevsky befriended Apollon Maykov and his brother Valerian. In 1846, on the recommendation of the poet Aleksey Pleshcheyev, he joined the socio-Christian Petrashevsky Circle, founded by Mikhail Petrashevsky, who had proposed social reforms in Russia. Mikhail Bakunin once wrote to Alexander Herzen that the group was "the most innocent and harmless company" and its members were "systematic opponents of all revolutionary goals and means". Dostoyevsky used the circle's library on Saturdays and Sundays and occasionally participated in their discussions on freedom from censorship and the abolition of serfdom.

In 1849, the first parts of Netochka Nezvanova, a novel Dostoyevsky had been planning since 1846, were published in Annals of the Fatherland, but his banishment ended the project. Dostoyevsky never attempted to complete it.

Siberian Exile (1849–1854)

The members of the Petrashevsky Circle were denounced to Liprandi, an official at the Ministry of International Affairs. Dostoyevsky was accused of reading works by Belinsky, including the banned Letter to Gogol, and of circulating copies of these and other works. Antonelli, the government agent who had reported the group, wrote in his statement that at least one of the papers criticised Russian politics and religion. Dostoyevsky responded to these charges by declaring that he had read the essays only "as a literary monument, neither more nor less"; he spoke of "personality and human egoism" rather than of politics. Even so, he and his fellow "conspirators" were arrested on 23 April 1849 at the request of Count A. Orlov and Emperor Nicolas I, who feared a revolution like the Decembrist revolt of 1825 in Russia and the Revolutions of 1848 in Europe. The members were held in the well-defended Peter and Paul Fortress, which housed the most dangerous convicts.

The case was discussed for four months by an investigative commission headed by the Tsar, with Adjutant General Ivan Nabokov, senator Count Pavel Gagarin, Count Vasili Dolgorukov, General Yakov Rostovtsev and General Leonty Dubelt, head of the secret police. They sentenced the members of the circle to death by firing squad, and the prisoners were taken to Semyonov Place in St Petersburg on 23 December 1849 where they were split into three-man groups. Dostoyevsky was the third in the second row; next to him stood Pleshcheyev and Durov. The execution was stayed when a cart delivered a letter from the Tsar commuting the sentence.

Dostoyevsky served four years of exile with hard labour at a katorga prison camp in Omsk, Siberia, followed by a term of compulsory military service. After a fourteen-day sleigh ride, the prisoners reached Tobolsk, a prisoner way station. Despite the circumstances, Dostoyevsky consoled the other prisoners, such as the Petrashevist Ivan Yastrzhembsky, who was surprised by Dostoyevsky's kindness and eventually abandoned his decision to commit suicide. In Tobolsk, the members received food and clothes from the Decembrist women, as well as several copies of the New Testament with a ten-ruble banknote inside each copy. Eleven days later, Dostoyevsky reached Omsk together with just one other member of the Petrashevsky Circle, the poet Sergei Durov. Dostoyevsky described his barracks:

In summer, intolerable closeness; in winter, unendurable cold. All the floors were rotten. Filth on the floors an inch thick; one could slip and fall ... We were packed like herrings in a barrel ... There was no room to turn around. From dusk to dawn it was impossible not to behave like pigs ... Fleas, lice, and black beetles by the bushel ...

Classified as "one of the most dangerous convicts", Dostoyevsky had his hands and feet shackled until his release. He was permitted to read nothing but his New Testament. In addition to his seizures, he had haemorrhoids, lost weight and was "burned by some fever, trembling and feeling too hot or too cold every night". The smell of the privy pervaded the entire building, and the small bathroom had to suffice for more than 200 people. Dostoyevsky was occasionally sent to the military hospital, where he read newspapers and Dickens novels. He was generally respected by the prisoners, but despised by some because of his xenophobic statements.

Release from Prison (1854–1865)

After his release on 14 February 1854, Dostoyevsky asked Mikhail to help him financially and to send him books by Vico, Guizot, Ranke, Hegel and Kant. The House of the Dead, based on his experience in prison, was published in 1861 in the journal Vremya – it was the first published novel about Russian prisons. Before moving in mid-March to Semipalatinsk, where he was forced to serve in the Siberian Army Corps of the Seventh Line Battalion, Dostoyevsky met geographer Pyotr Semyonov and ethnographer Shokan Walikhanuli. Around November 1854, he met Baron Alexander Egorovich Wrangel, an admirer of his books, who had attended the aborted execution. They both rented houses in the Cossack Garden outside Semipalatinsk. Wrangel remarked that Dostoyevsky "looked morose. His sickly, pale face was covered with freckles, and his blond hair was cut short. He was a little over average height and looked at me intensely with his sharp, grey-blue eyes. It was as if he were trying to look into my soul and discover what kind of man I was."

In Semipalatinsk, Dostoyevsky tutored several schoolchildren and came into contact with upper-class families, including that of Lieutenant-Colonel Belikhov, who used to invite him to read passages from newspapers and magazines. During a visit to Belikhov, Dostoyevsky met the family of Alexander Ivanovich Isaev and Maria Dmitrievna Isaeva and fell in love with the latter. Alexander Isaev took a new post in Kuznetsk, where he died in August 1855. Maria then moved with Dostoyevsky to Barnaul. In 1856 Dostoyevsky sent a letter through Wrangel to General Eduard Totleben, apologising for his activity in several utopian circles. As a result, he obtained the right to publish books and to marry, although he remained under police surveillance for the rest of his life. Maria married Dostoyevsky in Semipalatinsk on 7 February 1857, even though she had initially refused his marriage proposal, stating that they were not meant for each other and that his poor financial situation precluded marriage. Their family life was unhappy and she found it difficult to cope with his seizures. Describing their relationship, he wrote: "Because of her strange, suspicious and fantastic character, we were definitely not happy together, but we could not stop loving each other; and the more unhappy we were, the more attached to each other we became". They mostly lived apart. In 1859 he was released from military service because of deteriorating health and was granted permission to return to Russia, first to Tver, where he met his brother for the first time in ten years, and then to St Petersburg. "A Little Hero" (Dostoyevsky's only work completed in prison) appeared in a journal, but "Uncle's Dream" and "The Village of Stepanchikovo" were not published until 1860. Notes from the House of the Dead was released in Russky Mir (Russian World) in September 1860. "The Insulted and the Injured" was published in the new Vremya (Time) magazine, which had been created with the help of funds from his brother's cigarette factory.

Dostoyevsky travelled to western Europe for the first time on 7 June 1862, visiting Cologne, Berlin, Dresden, Wiesbaden, Belgium and Paris. In London he met Herzen and visited the Crystal Palace. He travelled with Nikolay Strakhov through Switzerland and several North Italian cities, including Turin, Livorno and Florence. He recorded his impressions of those trips in Winter Notes on Summer Impressions, in which he criticised capitalism, social modernisation, materialism, Catholicism and Protestantism.

From August to October 1863, Dostoyevsky made another trip to western Europe. He met his second love, Polina Suslova, in Paris and lost nearly all his money gambling in Wiesbaden and Baden-Baden. In 1864 his wife Maria and brother Mikhail died, and Dostoyevsky became the lone parent of his stepson Pasha and the sole supporter of his brother's family. The failure of Epoch, the magazine he had founded with Mikhail after the suppression of Vremya, worsened his financial situation, although the continued help of his relatives and friends averted bankruptcy.

Marriage and Honeymoon (1866–1871)

The first two parts of Crime and Punishment were published in January and February 1866 in the periodical The Russian Messenger, attracting at least 500 new subscribers to the magazine.

Dostoyevsky returned to Saint Petersburg in mid-September and promised his editor, Fyodor Stellovsky, that he would complete The Gambler, a short novel focused on gambling addiction, by November, although he had not yet begun writing it. One of Dostoyevsky's friends, Milyukov, advised him to hire a secretary. Dostoyevsky contacted stenographer Pavel Olkhin from Saint Petersburg, who recommended his pupil Anna Grigoryevna Snitkina. Her shorthand helped Dostoyevsky to complete The Gambler on 30 October, after 26 days' work. She remarked that Dostoyevsky was of average height but always tried to carry himself erect. "He had light brown, slightly reddish hair, he used some hair conditioner, and he combed his hair in a diligent way ... his eyes, they were different: one was dark brown; in the other, the pupil was so big that you could not see its color, [this was caused by an injury]. The strangeness of his eyes gave Dostoyevsky some mysterious appearance. His face was pale, and it looked unhealthy."

On 15 February 1867 Dostoyevsky married Snitkina in Trinity Cathedral, Saint Petersburg. The 7,000 rubles he had earned from Crime and Punishment did not cover their debts, forcing Anna to sell her valuables. On 14 April 1867 they began a delayed honeymoon in Germany with the money gained from the sale. They stayed in Berlin and visited the Gemäldegalerie Alte Meister, where he sought inspiration for his writing. They continued their trip through Germany, visiting Frankfurt, Darmstadt, Heidelberg and Karlsruhe and finally staying in Geneva. Their first child, Sonya, was conceived in Baden-Baden, and was born there on 5 March 1868. The baby died of pneumonia three months later, and Anna recalled how Dostoyevsky "wept and sobbed like a woman in despair". In September 1867, Dostoyevsky began work on The Idiot, and after a prolonged planning process that bore little resemblance to the published novel, he eventually managed to write the first 100 pages in only 23 days; the serialisation began in The Russian Messenger in January 1868. The couple moved from Geneva to Vevey and then to Milan, before continuing to Florence. The Idiot was completed there in January 1869, the final part appearing in The Russian Messenger in February 1869. Anna gave birth to their second daughter, Lyubov, on 26 September 1869 in Dresden. In April 1871, Dostoyevsky made a final visit to a gambling hall in Wiesbaden. Anna claimed that he stopped gambling after the birth of their second daughter, but this is a subject of debate.

After hearing news that the socialist revolutionary group "People's Vengeance" had murdered one of its own members, Ivan Ivanov, on 21 November 1869, Dostoyevsky began writing Demons. In 1871, Dostoyevsky and Anna travelled by train to Berlin. During the trip he burnt several manuscripts, including those of The Idiot, because he was concerned about potential problems with customs. The family arrived in Saint Petersburg on 8 July, marking the end of a honeymoon (originally planned for three months) that had lasted over four years.

Return to Russia (1871–1875)

Back in Russia in July 1871, the family was again in financial trouble and had to sell their remaining possessions. Their son Fyodor was born on 16 July, and they moved to an apartment near the Institute of Technology soon after. They hoped to cancel their large debts by selling their rental house in Peski, but difficulties with the tenant resulted in a relatively low selling price, and disputes with their creditors continued. Anna proposed that they raise money on her husband's copyrights and negotiate with the creditors to pay off their debts in installments.

Dostoyevsky revived his friendships with Maykov and Strakhov and made new acquaintances, including church politician Terty Filipov and the brothers Vsevolod and Vladimir Solovyov. Konstantin Pobedonostsev, future Imperial High Commissioner of the Most Holy Synod, influenced Dostoyevsky's political progression to conservatism. Around early 1872 the family spent several months in Staraya Russa, a town known for its mineral spa. Dostoyevsky's work was delayed when Anna's sister Maria Svatkovskaya died on 1 May 1872, either from typhus or malaria, and Anna developed an abscess on her throat.

The family returned to St Petersburg in September. Demons was finished on 26 November and released in January 1873 by the "Dostoyevsky Publishing Company", which was founded by Dostoyevsky and his wife. Although they only accepted cash payments and the bookshop was in their own apartment, the business was successful, and they sold around 3,000 copies of Demons. Anna managed the finances. Dostoyevsky proposed that they establish a new periodical, which would be called A Writer's Diary and would include a collection of essays, but funds were lacking, and the Diary was published in Vladimir Meshchersky's The Citizen, beginning on 1 January, in return for a salary of 3,000 rubles per year. In the summer of 1873, Anna returned to Staraya Russa with the children, while Dostoyevsky stayed in St Petersburg to continue with his Diary.

In March 1874 Dostoyevsky left The Citizen because of the stressful work and interference from the Russian bureaucracy. In his fifteen months with The Citizen, he had been taken to court twice: on 11 June 1873 for citing the words of Prince Meshchersky without permission, and again on 23 March 1874. Dostoyevsky offered to sell a new novel he had not yet begun to write to The Russian Messenger, but the magazine refused. Nikolay Nekrasov suggested that he publish A Writer's Diary in Notes of the Fatherland; he would receive 250 rubles for each printer's sheet – 100 more than the text's publication in The Russian Messenger would have earned. Dostoyevsky accepted. As his health began to decline, he consulted several doctors in St Petersburg and was advised to take a cure outside Russia. Around July, he reached Ems and consulted a physician, who diagnosed him with acute catarrh. During his stay he began The Adolescent. He returned to Saint Petersburg in late July.

Anna proposed that they spend the winter in Staraya Russa to allow Dostoyevsky to rest, although doctors had suggested a second visit to Ems because his health had previously improved there. On 10 August 1875 his son Alexey was born in Staraya Russa, and in mid-September the family returned to Saint Petersburg. Dostoyevsky finished The Adolescent at the end of 1875, although passages of it had been serialised in Notes of the Fatherland since January. The Adolescent chronicles the life of Arkady Dolgoruky, the illegitimate child of the landowner Versilov and a peasant mother. It deals primarily with the relationship between father and son, which became a frequent theme in Dostoyevsky's subsequent works.

Last Years (1876–1881)

In early 1876, Dostoyevsky continued work on his Diary. The book includes numerous essays and a few short stories about society, religion, politics and ethics. The collection sold more than twice as many copies as his previous books. Dostoyevsky received more letters from readers than ever before, and people of all ages and occupations visited him. With assistance from Anna's brother, the family bought a dacha in Staraya Russa. In the summer of 1876, Dostoyevsky began experiencing shortness of breath again. He visited Ems for a third time and was told that he might live for another 15 years if he moved to a healthier climate. When he returned to Russia, Tsar Alexander II ordered Dostoyevsky to visit his palace to present the Diary to him, and he asked him to educate his sons, Sergey and Paul. This visit further increased Dosteyevsky's circle of acquaintances. He was a frequent guest in several salons in Saint Petersburg and met many famous people, including Princess Sophia Tolstaya, Yakov Polonsky, Sergei Witte, Alexey Suvorin, Anton Rubinstein and Ilya Repin.

Dostoyevsky's health declined further, and in March 1877 he had four epileptic seizures. Rather than returning to Ems, he visited Maly Prikol, a manor near Kursk. While returning to St Petersburg to finalise his Diary, he visited Darovoye, where he had spent much of his childhood. In December he attended Nekrasov's funeral and gave a speech. He was appointed an honorary member of the Russian Academy of Sciences, from which he received an honorary certificate in February 1879. He declined an invitation to an international congress on copyright in Paris after his son Alyosha had a severe epileptic seizure and died on 16 May. The family later moved to the apartment where Dostoyevsky had written his first works. Around this time, he was elected to the board of directors of the Slavic Benevolent Society in Saint Petersburg. That summer, he was elected to the honorary committee of the Association Littéraire et Artistique Internationale, whose members included Victor Hugo, Ivan Turgenev, Paul Heyse, Alfred Tennyson, Anthony Trollope, Henry Longfellow, Ralph Waldo Emerson and Leo Tolstoy. Dostoyevsky made his fourth and final visit to Ems in early August 1879. He was diagnosed with early-stage pulmonary emphysema, which his doctor believed could be successfully managed, but not cured.

On 3 February 1880 Dostoyevsky was elected vice-president of the Slavic Benevolent Society, and he was invited to speak at the unveiling of the Pushkin memorial in Moscow. On 8 June he delivered his speech, giving an impressive performance that had a significant emotional impact on his audience. His speech was met with thunderous applause, and even his long-time rival Turgenev embraced him. Konstantin Staniukovich praised the speech in his essay "The Pushkin Anniversary and Dostoyevsky's Speech" in The Business, writing that "the language of Dostoyevsky's [Pushkin Speech] really looks like a sermon. He speaks with the tone of a prophet. He makes a sermon like a pastor; it is very deep, sincere, and we understand that he wants to impress the emotions of his listeners." The speech was criticised later by liberal political scientist Alexander Gradovsky, who thought that Dostoyevsky idolised "the people", and by conservative thinker Konstantin Leontiev, who, in his essay "On Universal Love", compared the speech to French utopian socialism. The attacks led to a further deterioration in his health.

On 25 January 1881, while searching for members of the terrorist organisation Narodnaya Volya ("The People's Will") who would soon assassinate Tsar Alexander II, the Tsar's secret police executed a search warrant in the apartment of one of Dostoyevsky's neighbours. On the following day, Dostoyevsky suffered a pulmonary haemorrhage. Anna denied that the search had caused it, saying that the haemorrhage had occurred after her husband had been looking for a dropped pen holder. After another haemorrhage, Anna called the doctors, who gave a poor prognosis. A third haemorrhage followed shortly afterwards.

Among Dostoyevsky's last words was his quotation of Matthew 3:14–15: "But John forbad him, saying, I have need to be baptised of thee, and comest thou to me? And Jesus answering said unto him, Suffer it to be so now: for thus it becometh us to fulfil all righteousness", and he finished with "Hear now—permit it. Do not restrain me!" When he died, his body was placed on a table, following Russian custom. He was interred in the Tikhvin Cemetery at the Alexander Nevsky Convent, near his favourite poets, Karamsin and Zhukovsky. It is unclear how many attended his funeral. According to one reporter, more than 100,000 mourners were present, while others describe attendance between 40,000 and 50,000. His tombstone is inscribed with lines from the New Testament:
Verily, verily, I say unto you, Except a corn of wheat fall into the ground and die, it abideth alone: but if it die, it bringeth forth much fruit. – John 12:24

Extramarital Affairs

Dostoyevsky had his first known affair with Avdotya Yakovlevna, whom he met in the Panayev circle in the early 1840s. He described her as educated, interested in literature, and a femme fatale. He admitted later that he was uncertain about their relationship. According to Anna Dostoyevskaya's memoirs, Dostoyevsky once asked his sister's sister-in-law, Yelena Ivanova, whether she would marry him, hoping to replace her mortally ill husband after he died, but she rejected his proposal. Dostoyevsky and Apollonia (Polina) Suslova had a short but intimate affair, which peaked in the winter of 1862–63. Suslova's dalliance with a Spaniard in late spring and Dostoyevsky's gambling addiction and age ended their relationship. He later described her in a letter to Nadezhda Suslova as a "great egoist. Her egoism and her vanity are colossal. She demands everything of other people, all the perfections, and does not pardon the slightest imperfection in the light of other qualities that one may possess", and later stated "I still love her, but I do not want to love her any more. She doesn't deserve this love ..." In 1858 Dostoyevsky had a romance with comic actress Aleksandra Ivanovna Schubert. Although she divorced Dostoyevsky's friend Stepan Yanovsky, she would not live with him. Dostoyevsky did not love her either, but they were probably good friends. She wrote that he "became very attracted to me".

Through a worker in Epoch, Dostoyevsky learned of the Russian-born Martha Brown (née Elizaveta Andreyevna Chlebnikova), who had had affairs with several westerners. Her relationship with Dostoyevsky is known only through letters written between November 1864 and January 1865. In 1865, Dostoyevsky met Anna Korvin-Krukovskaya. Their relationship is not verified; Anna Dostoyevskaya spoke of a good affair, but Korvin-Krukovskaya's sister, the mathematician Sofia Kovalevskaya, thought that Korvin-Krukovskaya had rejected him.

THE GRAND INQUISITOR

By
Feodor Dostoevsky
(Translation by H.P. Blavatsky)

[Dedicated by the Translator to those sceptics who clamour so loudly, both in print and private letters—"Show us the wonder-working 'Brothers,' let them come out publicly—and we will believe in them!"]

[The following is an extract from M. Dostoevsky's celebrated novel, The Brothers Karamazof, the last publication from the pen of the great Russian novelist, who died a few months ago, just as the concluding chapters appeared in print. Dostoevsky is beginning to be recognized as one of the ablest and profoundest among Russian writers. His characters are invariably typical portraits drawn from various classes of Russian society, strikingly life-like and realistic to the highest degree. The following extract is a cutting satire on modern theology generally and the Roman Catholic religion in particular. The idea is that Christ revisits earth, coming to Spain at the period of the Inquisition, and is at once arrested as a heretic by the Grand Inquisitor. One of the three brothers of the story, Ivan, a rank materialist and an atheist of the new school, is supposed to throw this conception into the form of a poem, which he describes to Alyosha—the youngest of the brothers, a young Christian mystic brought up by a "saint" in a monastery—as follows: (—Ed. Theosophist, Nov., 1881)]

"Quite impossible, as you see, to start without an introduction," laughed Ivan. "Well, then, I mean to place the event described in the poem in the sixteenth century, an age—as you must have been told at school—when it was the great fashion among poets to make the denizens and powers of higher worlds descend on earth and mix freely with mortals... In France all the notaries' clerks, and the monks in the cloisters as well, used to give grand performances, dramatic plays in which long scenes were enacted by the Madonna, the angels, the saints, Christ, and even by God Himself. In those days, everything was very artless and primitive. An instance of it may be found in Victor Hugo's drama, Notre Dame de Paris, where, at the Municipal Hall, a play called Le Bon Jugement de la Tres-sainte et Gracièuse Vierge Marie, is enacted in honour of Louis XI, in which the Virgin appears personally to pronounce her 'good judgment.' In Moscow, during the prepetrean period, performances of nearly the same character, chosen especially from the Old Testament, were also in great favour. Apart from such plays, the world was overflooded with mystical writings, 'verses'—the heroes of which were always selected from the ranks of angels, saints and other heavenly citizens answering to the devotional purposes of the age. The recluses of our monasteries, like the Roman Catholic monks, passed their time in translating, copying, and even producing original compositions upon such subjects, and that, remember, during the Tarter period!... In this connection, I am reminded of a poem compiled in a convent—a translation from the Greek, of course—called, 'The Travels of the Mother of God among the Damned,' with fitting illustrations and a boldness of conception inferior nowise to that of Dante. The 'Mother of God' visits hell, in company with the archangel Michael as her cicerone to guide her through the legions of the 'damned.' She sees them all, and is witness to their multifarious tortures. Among the many other exceedingly remarkably varieties of torments—every category of sinners having its own—there is one especially worthy of notice, namely a class of the 'damned' sentenced to gradually sink in a burning lake of brimstone and fire. Those whose sins cause them to sink so low that they no longer can rise to the surface are for ever forgotten by God, i.e., they fade out from the omniscient memory, says the poem—an expression, by the way, of an extraordinary profundity of thought, when closely analysed. The Virgin is terribly shocked, and falling down upon her knees in tears before the throne of God, begs that all she has seen in hell—all, all without exception, should have their sentences remitted to them. Her dialogue with God is colossally interesting. She supplicates, she will not leave Him. And when God, pointing to the pierced hands and feet of her Son, cries, 'How can I forgive His executioners?' She then commands that all the saints, martyrs, angels and archangels, should prostrate themselves with her before the Immutable and Changeless One and implore Him to change His wrath into mercy and—forgive them all. The poem closes upon her obtaining from God a compromise, a kind of yearly respite of tortures between Good Friday and Trinity, a chorus of the 'damned' singing loud praises to God from their 'bottomless pit,' thanking and telling Him:

> Thou art right, O Lord, very right,
> Thou hast condemned us justly.

"My poem is of the same character.

"In it, it is Christ who appears on the scene. True, He says nothing, but only appears and passes out of sight. Fifteen centuries have elapsed since He left the world with the distinct promise to return 'with power and great glory'; fifteen long centuries since His prophet cried, 'Prepare ye the way of the Lord!' since He Himself had foretold, while yet on earth, 'Of that day and hour knoweth no man, no, not the angels of heaven but my Father only.' But Christendom expects Him still. ...

"It waits for Him with the same old faith and the same emotion; aye, with a far greater faith, for fifteen centuries have rolled away since the last sign from heaven was sent to man,

> And blind faith remained alone
> To lull the trusting heart,
> As heav'n would send a sign no more.

"True, again, we have all heard of miracles being wrought ever since the 'age of miracles' passed away to return no more. We had, and still have, our saints credited with performing the most miraculous cures; and, if we can believe their biographers, there have been those among them who have been personally visited by the Queen of Heaven. But Satan sleepeth not, and the first germs of doubt, and ever-increasing unbelief in such wonders, already had begun to sprout in Christendom as early as the sixteenth century. It was just at that time that a new and terrible heresy first made its appearance in the north of Germany.* [*Luther's reform] A great star 'shining as it were a lamp... fell upon the fountains waters'... and 'they were made bitter.' This 'heresy' blasphemously denied 'miracles.' But those who had remained faithful believed all the more ardently, the tears of mankind ascended to Him as heretofore, and the Christian world was expecting Him as confidently as ever; they loved Him and hoped in Him, thirsted and hungered to suffer and die for Him just as many of them had done before.... So many centuries had weak, trusting humanity implored Him, crying with ardent faith and fervour: 'How long, O Lord, holy and true, dost Thou not come!' So many long centuries hath it vainly appealed to Him, that at last, in His inexhaustible compassion, He consenteth to answer the prayer.... He decideth that once more, if it were but for one short hour, the people—His long-suffering, tortured, fatally sinful, his loving and child-like, trusting people—shall behold Him again. The scene of action is placed by me in Spain, at Seville, during that terrible period of the Inquisition, when, for the greater glory of God, stakes were flaming all over the country.

     Burning wicked heretics,
    In grand auto-da-fes.

"This particular visit has, of course, nothing to do with the promised Advent, when, according to the programme, 'after the tribulation of those days,' He will appear 'coming in the clouds of heaven.' For, that 'coming of the Son of Man,' as we are informed, will take place as suddenly 'as the lightning cometh out of the east and shineth even unto the west.' No; this once, He desired to come unknown, and appear among His children, just when the bones of the heretics, sentenced to be burnt alive, had commenced crackling at the flaming stakes. Owing to His limitless mercy, He mixes once more with mortals and in the same form in which He was wont to appear fifteen centuries ago. He descends, just at the very moment when before king, courtiers, knights, cardinals, and the fairest dames of court, before the whole population of Seville, upwards of a hundred wicked heretics are being roasted, in a magnificent auto-da-fe ad majorem Dei gloriam, by the order of the powerful Cardinal Grand Inquisitor.

"He comes silently and unannounced; yet all—how strange—yea, all recognize Him, at once! The population rushes towards Him as if propelled by some irresistible force; it surrounds, throngs, and presses around, it follows Him.... Silently, and with a smile of boundless compassion upon His lips, He crosses the dense crowd, and moves softly on. The Sun of Love burns in His heart, and warm rays of Light, Wisdom and Power beam forth from His eyes, and pour down their waves upon the swarming multitudes of the rabble assembled around, making their hearts vibrate with returning love. He extends His hands over their heads, blesses them, and from mere contact with Him, aye, even with His garments, a healing power goes forth. An old man, blind from his birth, cries, 'Lord, heal me, that I may see Thee!' and the scales falling off the closed eyes, the blind man beholds Him... The crowd weeps for joy, and kisses the ground upon which He treads. Children strew flowers along His path and sing to Him, 'Hosanna!' It is He, it is Himself, they say to each other, it must be He, it can be none other but He! He pauses at the portal of the old cathedral, just as a wee white coffin is carried in, with tears and great lamentations. The lid is off, and in the coffin lies the body of a fair-child, seven years old, the only child of an eminent citizen of the city. The little corpse lies buried in flowers. 'He will raise the child to life!' confidently shouts the crowd to the weeping mother. The officiating priest who had come to meet the funeral procession, looks perplexed, and frowns. A loud cry is suddenly heard, and the bereaved mother prostrates herself at His feet. 'If it be Thou, then bring back my child to life!' she cries beseechingly. The procession halts, and the little coffin is gently lowered at his feet. Divine compassion beams forth from His eyes, and as He looks at the child, His lips are heard to whisper once more, 'Talitha Cumi'—and 'straightway the damsel arose.' The child rises in her coffin. Her little hands still hold the nosegay of white roses which after death was placed in them, and, looking round with large astonished eyes she smiles sweetly .... The crowd is violently excited. A terrible commotion rages among them, the populace shouts and loudly weeps, when suddenly, before the cathedral door, appears the Cardinal Grand Inquisitor himself.... He is tall, gaunt-looking old man of nearly four-score years and ten, with a stern, withered face, and deeply sunken eyes, from the cavity of which glitter two fiery sparks. He has laid aside his gorgeous cardinal's robes in which he had appeared before the people at the auto da-fe of the enemies of the Romish Church, and is now clad in his old, rough, monkish cassock. His sullen assistants and slaves of the 'holy guard' are following at a distance. He pauses before the crowd and observes. He has seen all. He has witnessed the placing of the little coffin at His feet, the calling back to life. And now, his dark, grim face has grown still darker; his bushy grey eyebrows nearly meet, and his sunken eye flashes with sinister light. Slowly raising his finger, he commands his minions to arrest Him....

"Such is his power over the well-disciplined, submissive and now trembling people, that the thick crowds immediately give way, and scattering before the guard, amid dead silence and without one breath of protest, allow them to lay their sacrilegious hands upon the stranger and lead Him away.... That same populace, like one man, now bows its head to the ground before the old Inquisitor, who blesses it and slowly moves onward. The guards conduct their prisoner to the ancient building of the Holy Tribunal; pushing Him into a narrow, gloomy, vaulted prison-cell, they lock Him in and retire....

"The day wanes, and night—a dark, hot breathless Spanish night—creeps on and settles upon the city of Seville. The air smells of laurels and orange blossoms. In the Cimmerian darkness of the old Tribunal Hall the iron door of the cell is suddenly thrown open, and the Grand

Inquisitor, holding a dark lantern, slowly stalks into the dungeon. He is alone, and, as the heavy door closes behind him, he pauses at the threshold, and, for a minute or two, silently and gloomily scrutinizes the Face before him. At last approaching with measured steps, he sets his lantern down upon the table and addresses Him in these words:

"'It is Thou! ... Thou!' ... Receiving no reply, he rapidly continues: 'Nay, answer not; be silent! ... And what couldst Thou say? ... I know but too well Thy answer.... Besides, Thou hast no right to add one syllable to that which was already uttered by Thee before.... Why shouldst Thou now return, to impede us in our work? For Thou hast come but for that only, and Thou knowest it well. But art Thou as well aware of what awaits Thee in the morning? I do not know, nor do I care to know who thou mayest be: be it Thou or only thine image, to-morrow I will condemn and burn Thee on the stake, as the most wicked of all the heretics; and that same people, who to-day were kissing Thy feet, to-morrow at one bend of my finger, will rush to add fuel to Thy funeral pile... Wert Thou aware of this?' he adds, speaking as if in solemn thought, and never for one instant taking his piercing glance off the meek Face before him."....

"I can hardly realize the situation described—what is all this, Ivan?" suddenly interrupted Alyosha, who had remained silently listening to his brother. "Is this an extravagant fancy, or some mistake of the old man, an impossible quid pro quo?"

"Let it be the latter, if you like," laughed Ivan, "since modern realism has so perverted your taste that you feel unable to realize anything from the world of fancy.... Let it be a quid pro quo, if you so choose it. Again, the Inquisitor is ninety years old, and he might have easily gone mad with his one idee fixe of power; or, it might have as well been a delirious vision, called forth by dying fancy, overheated by the auto-da-fe of the hundred heretics in that forenoon.... But what matters for the poem, whether it was a quid pro quo or an uncontrollable fancy? The question is, that the old man has to open his heart; that he must give out his thought at last; and that the hour has come when he does speak it out, and says loudly that which for ninety years he has kept secret within his own breast."

"And his prisoner, does He never reply? Does He keep silent, looking at him, without saying a word?"

"Of course; and it could not well be otherwise," again retorted Ivan. "The Grand Inquisitor begins from his very first words by telling Him that He has no right to add one syllable to that which He had said before. To make the situation clear at once, the above preliminary monologue is intended to convey to the reader the very fundamental idea which underlies Roman Catholicism—as well as I can convey it, his words mean, in short: 'Everything was given over by Thee to the Pope, and everything now rests with him alone; Thou hast no business to return and thus hinder us in our work.' In this sense the Jesuits not only talk but write likewise.

"'Hast thou the right to divulge to us a single one of the mysteries of that world whence Thou comest?' enquires of Him my old Inquisitor, and forthwith answers for Him. 'Nay, Thou has no such right. For, that would be adding to that which was already said by Thee before; hence depriving people of that freedom for which Thou hast so stoutly stood up while yet on earth.... Anything new that Thou would now proclaim would have to be regarded as an attempt to interfere with that freedom of choice, as it would come as a new and a miraculous revelation superseding the old revelation of fifteen hundred years ago, when Thou didst so repeatedly tell the people: "The truth shall make you free." Behold then, Thy "free" people now!' adds the old man with sombre irony. 'Yea!... it has cost us dearly.' he continues, sternly looking at his victim. 'But we have at last accomplished our task, and—in Thy name.... For fifteen long centuries we had to toil and suffer owing to that "freedom": but now we have prevailed and our work is done, and well and strongly it is done. ....Believest not Thou it is so very strong? ... And why should Thou look at me so meekly as if I were not worthy even of Thy indignation?... Know then, that now, and only now, Thy people feel fully sure and satisfied of their freedom; and that only since they have themselves and of their own free will delivered that freedom unto our hands by placing it submissively at our feet. But then, that is what we have done. Is it that which Thou has striven for? Is this the kind of "freedom" Thou has promised them?'"

"Now again, I do not understand," interrupted Alyosha. "Does the old man mock and laugh?"

"Not in the least. He seriously regards it as a great service done by himself, his brother monks and Jesuits, to humanity, to have conquered and subjected unto their authority that freedom, and boasts that it was done but for the good of the world. 'For only now,' he says (speaking of the Inquisition) 'has it become possible to us, for the first time, to give a serious thought to human happiness. Man is born a rebel, and can rebels be ever happy?... Thou has been fairly warned of it, but evidently to no use, since Thou hast rejected the only means which could make mankind happy; fortunately at Thy departure Thou hast delivered the task to us.... Thou has promised, ratifying the pledge by Thy own words, in words giving us the right to bind and unbind... and surely, Thou couldst not think of depriving us of it now!'"

"But what can he mean by the words, 'Thou has been fairly warned'?" asked Alexis.

"These words give the key to what the old man has to say for his justification... But listen—

"'The terrible and wise spirit, the spirit of self annihilation and non-being,' goes on the Inquisitor, 'the great spirit of negation conversed with Thee in the wilderness, and we are told that he "tempted" Thee... Was it so? And if it were so, then it is impossible to utter anything more truthful than what is contained in his three offers, which Thou didst reject, and which are usually called "temptations." Yea; if ever there was on earth a genuine striking wonder produced, it was on that day of Thy three temptations, and it is precisely in these three short sentences that the marvelous miracle is contained. If it were possible that they should vanish and disappear for ever, without leaving any trace, from the record and from the memory of man, and that it should become necessary again to devise, invent, and make them reappear in Thy history once more, thinkest Thou that all the world's sages, all the legislators, initiates, philosophers and thinkers, if called upon to frame three questions which should, like these, besides answering the magnitude of the event, express in three short sentences the whole future history of this our world and of mankind—dost Thou believe, I ask Thee, that all their combined efforts could ever create anything equal in power and depth of thought to the three propositions offered Thee by the powerful and all-wise spirit in the wilderness? Judging of them by their marvelous aptness alone, one can at once perceive that they emanated not from a finite, terrestrial intellect, but indeed, from the Eternal and the Absolute. In these three offers we find, blended into one and foretold to us, the complete subsequent history of man; we are shown three images, so to say, uniting in them all the future axiomatic, insoluble problems and contradictions of human nature, the world over. In those days, the wondrous wisdom contained in them was not made so apparent as it is now, for futurity remained still veiled; but now, when fifteen centuries have elapsed, we see that everything in these three questions is so marvelously foreseen and foretold, that to add to, or to take away from, the prophecy one jot, would be absolutely impossible!

"'Decide then thyself.' sternly proceeded the Inquisitor, 'which of ye twain was right: Thou who didst reject, or he who offered? Remember the subtle meaning of question the first, which runs thus: Wouldst Thou go into the world empty-handed? Would Thou venture thither with Thy vague and undefined promise of freedom, which men, dull and unruly as they are by nature, are unable so much as to understand, which they avoid and fear?—for never was there anything more unbearable to the human race than personal freedom! Dost Thou see these stones in the desolate and glaring wilderness? Command that these stones be made bread—and mankind will run after Thee, obedient and grateful like a herd of cattle. But even then it will be ever diffident and trembling, lest Thou should take away Thy hand, and they lose thereby their bread! Thou didst refuse to accept the offer for fear of depriving men of their free choice; for where is there freedom of choice where men are bribed with bread? Man shall not live by bread alone—was Thine answer. Thou knewest not, it seems, that it was precisely in the name of that earthly bread that the terrestrial spirit would one day rise against, struggle with, and finally conquer Thee, followed by the hungry multitudes shouting: "Who is like unto that Beast, who maketh fire come down from heaven upon the earth!" Knowest Thou not that, but a few centuries hence, and the whole of mankind will have proclaimed in its wisdom and through its mouthpiece, Science, that there is no more crime, hence no more sin on earth, but only hungry people? "Feed us first and then command us to be virtuous!" will be the words written upon the banner lifted against Thee—a banner which shall destroy Thy Church to its very foundations, and in the place of Thy Temple shall raise once more the terrible Tower of Babel; and though its building be left unfinished, as was that of the first one, yet the fact will remain recorded that Thou couldst, but

wouldst not, prevent the attempt to build that new tower by accepting the offer, and thus saving mankind a millennium of useless suffering on earth. And it is to us that the people will return again. They will search for us catacombs, as we shall once more be persecuted and martyred—and they will begin crying unto us: "Feed us, for they who promised us the fire from heaven have deceived us!" It is then that we will finish building their tower for them. For they alone who feed them shall finish it, and we shall feed them in Thy name, and lying to them that it is in that name. Oh, never, never, will they learn to feed themselves without our help! No science will ever give them bread so long as they remain free, so long as they refuse to lay that freedom at our feet, and say: "Enslave, but feed us!" That day must come when men will understand that freedom and daily bread enough to satisfy all are unthinkable and can never be had together, as men will never be able to fairly divide the two among themselves. And they will also learn that they can never be free, for they are weak, vicious, miserable nonentities born wicked and rebellious. Thou has promised to them the bread of life, the bread of heaven; but I ask Thee again, can that bread ever equal in the sight of the weak and the vicious, the ever ungrateful human race, their daily bread on earth? And even supposing that thousands and tens of thousands follow Thee in the name of, and for the sake of, Thy heavenly bread, what will become of the millions and hundreds of millions of human beings to weak to scorn the earthly for the sake of Thy heavenly bread? Or is it but those tens of thousands chosen among the great and the mighty, that are so dear to Thee, while the remaining millions, innumerable as the grains of sand in the seas, the weak and the loving, have to be used as material for the former? No, no! In our sight and for our purpose the weak and the lowly are the more dear to us. True, they are vicious and rebellious, but we will force them into obedience, and it is they who will admire us the most. They will regard us as gods, and feel grateful to those who have consented to lead the masses and bear their burden of freedom by ruling over them—so terrible will that freedom at last appear to men! Then we will tell them that it is in obedience to Thy will and in Thy name that we rule over them. We will deceive them once more and lie to them once again—for never, never more will we allow Thee to come among us. In this deception we will find our suffering, for we must needs lie eternally, and never cease to lie!
"Such is the secret meaning of "temptation" the first, and that is what Thou didst reject in the wilderness for the sake of that freedom which Thou didst prize above all. Meanwhile Thy tempter's offer contained another great world-mystery. By accepting the "bread," Thou wouldst have satisfied and answered a universal craving, a ceaseless longing alive in the heart of every individual human being, lurking in the breast of collective mankind, that most perplexing problem—"whom or what shall we worship?" There exists no greater or more painful anxiety for a man who has freed himself from all religious bias, than how he shall soonest find a new object or idea to worship. But man seeks to bow before that only which is recognized by the greater majority, if not by all his fellow-men, as having a right to be worshipped; whose rights are so

unquestionable that men agree unanimously to bow down to it. For the chief concern of these miserable creatures is not to find and worship the idol of their own choice, but to discover that which all others will believe in, and consent to bow down to in a mass. It is that instinctive need of having a worship in common that is the chief suffering of every man, the chief concern of mankind from the beginning of times. It is for that universality of religious worship that people destroyed each other by sword. Creating gods unto themselves, they forwith began appealing to each other: "Abandon your deities, come and bow down to ours, or death to ye and your idols!" And so will they do till the end of this world; they will do so even then, when all the gods themselves have disappeared, for then men will prostrate themselves before and worship some idea. Thou didst know, Thou couldst not be ignorant of, that mysterious fundamental principle in human nature, and still thou hast rejected the only absolute banner offered Thee, to which all the nations would remain true, and before which all would have bowed—the banner of earthly bread, rejected in the name of freedom and of "bread in the kingdom of God"! Behold, then, what Thou hast done furthermore for that "freedom's" sake! I repeat to Thee, man has no greater anxiety in life than to find some one to whom he can make over that gift of freedom with which the unfortunate creature is born. But he alone will prove capable of silencing and quieting their consciences, that shall succeed in possessing himself of the freedom of men. With "daily bread" an irresistible power was offered Thee: show a man "bread" and he will follow Thee, for what can he resist less than the attraction of bread? But if, at the same time, another succeed in possessing himself of his conscience—oh! then even Thy bread will be forgotten, and man will follow him who seduced his conscience. So far Thou wert right. For the mystery of human being does not solely rest in the desire to live, but in the problem—for what should one live at all? Without a clear perception of his reasons for living, man will never consent to live, and will rather destroy himself than tarry on earth, though he be surrounded with bread. This is the truth. But what has happened? Instead of getting hold of man's freedom, Thou has enlarged it still more! Hast Thou again forgotten that to man rest and even death are preferable to a free choice between the knowledge of Good and Evil? Nothing seems more seductive in his eyes than freedom of conscience, and nothing proves more painful. And behold! instead of laying a firm foundation whereon to rest once for all man's conscience, Thou hast chosen to stir up in him all that is abnormal, mysterious, and indefinite, all that is beyond human strength, and has acted as if Thou never hadst any love for him, and yet Thou wert He who came to "lay down His life for His friends!" Thou hast burdened man's soul with anxieties hitherto unknown to him. Thirsting for human love freely given, seeking to enable man, seduced and charmed by Thee, to follow Thy path of his own free-will, instead of the old and wise law which held him in subjection, Thou hast given him the right henceforth to choose and freely decide what is good and bad for him, guided but by Thine image in his heart. But hast Thou never dreamt of the probability, nay, of the certainty, of that same man one day rejected finally, and controverting even Thine image and Thy truth, once he would find himself laden with such a terrible burden as freedom of choice? That a time would surely come when men would exclaim that Truth and Light cannot be in Thee, for no one could have left them in a greater perplexity and mental suffering than Thou has done, lading them with so many cares and insoluble problems. Thus, it is Thyself who hast laid the foundation for the destruction of Thine own kingdom and no one but Thou is to be blamed for it.

"'Meantime, every chance of success was offered Thee. There are three Powers, three unique Forces upon earth, capable of conquering for ever by charming the conscience of these weak rebels—men—for their own good; and these Forces are: Miracle, Mystery and Authority. Thou hast rejected all the three, and thus wert the first to set them an example. When the terrible and all-wise spirit placed Thee on a pinnacle of the temple and said unto Thee, "If Thou be the son of God, cast Thyself down, for it is written, He shall give His angels charge concerning Thee: and in their hands they shall bear Thee up, lest at any time Thou dash Thy foot against a stone!"—for thus Thy faith in Thy father should have been made evident, Thou didst refuse to accept his suggestion and didst not follow it. Oh, undoubtedly, Thou didst act in this with all the magnificent pride of a god, but then men—that weak and rebel race—are they also gods, to understand Thy refusal? Of course, Thou didst well know that by taking one single step forward, by making the slightest motion to throw Thyself down, Thou wouldst have tempted "the Lord Thy God," lost suddenly all faith in Him, and dashed Thyself to atoms against that same earth which Thou camest to save, and thus wouldst have allowed the wise spirit which tempted Thee to triumph and rejoice. But, then, how many such as Thee are to be found on this globe, I ask Thee? Couldst Thou ever for a moment imagine that men would have the same strength to resist such a temptation? Is human nature calculated to reject miracle, and trust, during the most terrible moments in life, when the most momentous, painful and perplexing problems struggle within man's soul, to the free decisions of his heart for the true solution? Oh, Thou knewest well that that action of Thine would remain recorded in books for ages to come, reaching to the confines of the globe, and Thy hope was, that following Thy example, man would remain true to his God, without needing any miracle to keep his faith alive! But Thou knewest not, it seems, that no sooner would man reject miracle than he would reject God likewise, for he seeketh less God than "a sign" from Him. And thus, as it is beyond the power of man to remain without miracles, so, rather than live without, he will create for himself new wonders of his own making; and he will bow to and worship the soothsayer's miracles, the old witch's sorcery, were he a rebel, a heretic, and an atheist a hundred times over. Thy refusal to come down from the cross when people, mocking and wagging their heads were saying to Thee—"Save Thyself if Thou be the son of God, and we will believe in Thee," was due to the same determination—not to enslave man through miracle, but to obtain faith in Thee freely and apart from any miraculous influence. Thou thirstest for free and uninfluenced love, and refuses the

passionate adoration of the slave before a Potency which would have subjected his will once for ever. Thou judgest of men too highly here, again, for though rebels they be, they are born slaves and nothing more. Behold, and judge of them once more, now that fifteen centuries have elapsed since that moment. Look at them, whom Thou didst try to elevate unto Thee! I swear man is weaker and lower than Thou hast ever imagined him to be! Can he ever do that which Thou art said to have accomplished? By valuing him so highly Thou hast acted as if there were no love for him in Thine heart, for Thou hast demanded of him more than he could ever give—Thou, who lovest him more than Thyself! Hadst Thou esteemed him less, less wouldst Thou have demanded of him, and that would have been more like love, for his burden would have been made thereby lighter. Man is weak and cowardly. What matters it, if he now riots and rebels throughout the world against our will and power, and prides himself upon that rebellion? It is but the petty pride and vanity of a school-boy. It is the rioting of little children, getting up a mutiny in the class-room and driving their schoolmaster out of it. But it will not last long, and when the day of their triumph is over, they will have to pay dearly for it. They will destroy the temples and raze them to the ground, flooding the earth with blood. But the foolish children will have to learn some day that, rebels though they be and riotous from nature, they are too weak to maintain the spirit of mutiny for any length of time. Suffused with idiotic tears, they will confess that He who created them rebellious undoubtedly did so but to mock them. They will pronounce these words in despair, and such blasphemous utterances will but add to their misery—for human nature cannot endure blasphemy, and takes her own revenge in the end.
"'And thus, after all Thou has suffered for mankind and its freedom, the present fate of men may be summed up in three words: Unrest, Confusion, Misery! Thy great prophet John records in his vision, that he saw, during the first resurrection of the chosen servants of God—"the number of them which were sealed" in their foreheads, "twelve thousand" of every tribe. But were they, indeed, as many? Then they must have been gods, not men. They had shared Thy Cross for long years, suffered scores of years' hunger and thirst in dreary wildernesses and deserts, feeding upon locusts and roots—and of these children of free love for Thee, and self-sacrifice in Thy name, Thou mayest well feel proud. But remember that these are but a few thousands—of gods, not men; and how about all others? And why should the weakest be held guilty for not being able to endure what the strongest have endured? Why should a soul incapable of containing such terrible gifts be punished for its weakness? Didst Thou really come to, and for, the "elect" alone? If so, then the mystery will remain for ever mysterious to our finite minds. And if a mystery, then were we right to proclaim it as one, and preach it, teaching them that neither their freely given love to Thee nor freedom of conscience were essential, but only that incomprehensible mystery which they must blindly obey even against the dictates of their conscience. Thus did we. We corrected and improved Thy teaching and based it upon "Miracle, Mystery, and Authority." And men rejoiced at

finding themselves led once more like a herd of cattle, and at finding their hearts at last delivered of the terrible burden laid upon them by Thee, which caused them so much suffering. Tell me, were we right in doing as we did. Did not we show our great love for humanity, by realizing in such a humble spirit its helplessness, by so mercifully lightening its great burden, and by permitting and remitting for its weak nature every sin, provided it be committed with our authorization? For what, then, hast Thou come again to trouble us in our work? And why lookest Thou at me so penetratingly with Thy meek eyes, and in such a silence? Rather shouldst Thou feel wroth, for I need not Thy love, I reject it, and love Thee not, myself. Why should I conceal the truth from Thee? I know but too well with whom I am now talking! What I had to say was known to Thee before, I read it in Thine eye. How should I conceal from Thee our secret? If perchance Thou wouldst hear it from my own lips, then listen: We are not with Thee, but with him, and that is our secret! For centuries have we abandoned Thee to follow him, yes—eight centuries. Eight hundred years now since we accepted from him the gift rejected by Thee with indignation; that last gift which he offered Thee from the high mountain when, showing all the kingdoms of the world and the glory of them, he saith unto Thee: "All these things will I give Thee, if Thou will fall down and worship me!" We took Rome from him and the glaive of Caesar, and declared ourselves alone the kings of this earth, its sole kings, though our work is not yet fully accomplished. But who is to blame for it? Our work is but in its incipient stage, but it is nevertheless started. We may have long to wait until its culmination, and mankind have to suffer much, but we shall reach the goal some day, and become sole Caesars, and then will be the time to think of universal happiness for men.

"'Thou couldst accept the glaive of Caesar Thyself; why didst Thou reject the offer? By accepting from the powerful spirit his third offer Thou would have realized every aspiration man seeketh for himself on earth; man would have found a constant object for worship; one to deliver his conscience up to, and one that should unite all together into one common and harmonious ant-hill; for an innate necessity for universal union constitutes the third and final affliction of mankind. Humanity as a whole has ever aspired to unite itself universally. Many were, the great nations with great histories, but the greater they were, the more unhappy they felt, as they felt the stronger necessity of a universal union among men. Great conquerors, like Timoor and Tchengis-Khan, passed like a cyclone upon the face of the earth in their efforts to conquer the universe, but even they, albeit unconsciously, expressed the same aspiration towards universal and common union. In accepting the kingdom of the world and Caesar's purple, one would found a universal kingdom and secure to mankind eternal peace. And who can rule mankind better than those who have possessed themselves of man's conscience, and hold in their hand man's daily bread? Having accepted Caesar's glaive and purple, we had, of course, but to deny Thee, to henceforth follow him alone. Oh, centuries of intellectual riot and rebellious free thought are yet before us, and their science will end by anthropophagy, for having begun to build their Babylonian tower without our help they will have to end by anthropophagy. But it is precisely at that time that the Beast will crawl up to us in full submission, and lick the scles of our feet, and sprinkle them with tears of blood and we shall sit upon the scarlet-colored Beast, and lifting up high the golden cup "full of abomination and filthiness," shall show written upon it the word "Mystery"! But it is only then that men will see the beginning of a kingdom of peace and happiness. Thou art proud of Thine own elect, but Thou has none other but these elect, and we—we will give rest to all. But that is not the end. Many are those among thine elect and the laborers of Thy vineyard, who, tired of waiting for Thy coming, already have carried and will yet carry, the great fervor of their hearts and their spiritual strength into another field, and will end by lifting up against Thee Thine own banner of freedom. But it is Thyself Thou hast to thank. Under our rule and sway all will be happy, and will neither rebel nor destroy each other as they did while under Thy free banner. Oh, we will take good care to prove to them that they will become absolutely free only when they have abjured their freedom in our favor and submit to us absolutely. Thinkest Thou we shall be right or still lying? They will convince themselves of our rightness, for they will see what a depth of degrading slavery and strife that liberty of Thine has led them into. Liberty, Freedom of Thought and Conscience, and Science will lead them into such impassable chasms, place them face to face before such wonders and insoluble mysteries, that some of them—more rebellious and ferocious than the rest—will destroy themselves; others—rebellious but weak—will destroy each other; while the remainder, weak, helpless and miserable, will crawl back to our feet and cry: "'Yes; right were ye, oh Fathers of Jesus; ye alone are in possession of His mystery, and we return to you, praying that ye save us from ourselves!" Receiving their bread from us, they will clearly see that we take the bread from them, the bread made by their own hands, but to give it back to them in equal shares and that without any miracle; and having ascertained that, though we have not changed stones into bread, yet bread they have, while every other bread turned verily in their own hands into stones, they will be only to glad to have it so. Until that day, they will never be happy. And who is it that helped the most to blind them, tell me? Who separated the flock and scattered it over ways unknown if it be not Thee? But we will gather the sheep once more and subject them to our will for ever. We will prove to them their own weakness and make them humble again, whilst with Thee they have learnt but pride, for Thou hast made more of them than they ever were worth. We will give them that quiet, humble happiness, which alone benefits such weak, foolish creatures as they are, and having once had proved to them their weakness, they will become timid and obedient, and gather around us as chickens around their hen. They will wonder at and feel a superstitious admiration for us, and feel proud to be led by men so powerful and wise that a handful of them can subject a flock a thousand millions strong. Gradually men will begin to fear us. They will nervously dread our slightest anger, their intellects will weaken, their eyes become as easily accessible to tears as those of children and women; but we will teach them an easy transition from grief and tears to laughter, childish joy and mirthful song. Yes; we will make them work like slaves, but during their recreation hours they shall have an innocent child-like life, full of play and merry laughter. We will even permit them sin, for, weak and helpless, they will feel the more love for us for permitting them to indulge in it. We will tell them that every kind of sin will be remitted to them, so long as it is done with our permission; that we take all these sins upon ourselves, for we so love the world, that we are even willing to sacrifice our souls for its satisfaction. And, appearing before them in the light of their scapegoats and redeemers, we shall be adored the more for it. They will have no secrets from us. It will rest with us to permit them to live with their wives and concubines, or to forbid them, to have children or remain childless, either way depending on the degree of their obedience to us; and they will submit most joyfully to us the most agonizing secrets of their souls—all, all will they lay down at our feet, and we will authorize and remit them all in Thy name, and they will believe us and accept our mediation with rapture, as it will deliver them from their greatest anxiety and torture—that of having to decide freely for themselves. And all will be happy, all except the one or two hundred thousands of their rulers. For it is but we, we the keepers of the great Mystery who will be miserable. There will be thousands of millions of happy infants, and one hundred thousand martyrs who have taken upon themselves the curse of knowledge of good and evil. Peaceable will be their end, and peacefully will they die, in Thy name, to find behind the portals of the grave—but death. But we will keep the secret inviolate, and deceive them for their own good with the mirage of life eternal in Thy kingdom. For, were there really anything like life beyond the grave, surely it would never fall to the lot of such as they! People tell us and prophesy of Thy coming and triumphing once more on earth; of Thy appearing with the army of Thy elect, with Thy proud and mighty ones; but we will answer Thee that they have saved but themselves while we have saved all. We are also threatened with the great disgrace which awaits the whore, "Babylon the great, the mother of harlots"—who sits upon the Beast, holding in her hands the Mystery, the word written upon her forehead; and we are told that the weak ones, the lambs shall rebel against her and shall make her desolate and naked. But then will I arise, and point out to Thee the thousands of millions of happy infants free from any sin. And we who have taken their sins upon us, for their own good, shall stand before Thee and say: "Judge us if Thou canst and darest!" Know then that I fear Thee not. Know that I too have lived in the dreary wilderness, where I fed upon locusts and roots, that I too have blessed freedom with which thou hast blessed men, and that I too have once prepared to join the ranks of Thy elect, the proud and the mighty. But I awoke from my delusion and refused since then to serve insanity. I returned to join the legion of those who corrected Thy mistakes. I left the proud and returned to the really humble, and for their own happiness. What I now tell thee will come to pass, and our kingdom shall be built, I tell Thee not later than to-morrow Thou shalt see that obedient flock which at one simple motion of my hand will rush to add burning coals to Thy stake, on which I will burn Thee for having dared to come and trouble us in our work. For, if there ever was one who deserved more than any of the others our inquisitorial fires—it is Thee! To-morrow I will burn Thee. Dixi'."

Ivan paused. He had entered into the situation and had spoken with great animation, but now he suddenly burst out laughing.

"But all that is absurd!" suddenly exclaimed Alyosha, who had hitherto listened perplexed and agitated but in profound silence. "Your poem is a glorification of Christ, not an accusation, as you, perhaps, meant to be. And who will believe you when you speak of 'freedom'? Is it thus that we Christians must understand it? It is Rome (not all Rome, for that would be unjust), but the worst of the Roman Catholics, the Inquisitors and Jesuits, that you have been exposing! Your Inquisitor is an impossible character. What are these sins they are taking upon themselves? Who are those keepers of mystery who took upon themselves a curse for the good of mankind? Who ever met them? We all know the Jesuits, and no one has a good word to say in their favor; but when were they as you depict them? Never, never! The Jesuits are merely a Romish army making ready for their future temporal kingdom, with a mitred emperor—a Roman high priest at their head. That is their ideal and object, without any mystery or elevated suffering. The most prosaic thirsting for power, for the sake of the mean and earthly pleasures of life, a desire to enslave their fellow-men, something like our late system of serfs, with themselves at the head as landed proprietors—that is all that they can be accused of. They may not believe in God, that is also possible, but your suffering Inquisitor is simply—a fancy!"

"Hold, hold!" interrupted Ivan, smiling. "Do not be so excited. A fancy, you say; be it so! Of course, it is a fancy. But stop. Do you really imagine that all this Catholic movement during the last centuries is naught but a desire for power for the mere purpose of 'mean pleasures'? Is this what your Father Paissiy taught you?"

"No, no, quite the reverse, for Father Paissiy once told me something very similar to what you yourself say, though, of course, not that—something quite different," suddenly added Alexis, blushing.

"A precious piece of information, notwithstanding your 'not that.' I ask you, why should the Inquisitors and the Jesuits of your imagination live but for the attainment of 'mean material pleasures?' Why should there not be found among them one single genuine martyr suffering under a great and holy idea and loving humanity with all his heart? Now let us suppose that among all these Jesuits thirsting and hungering but after 'mean material pleasures' there may be one, just one like my old Inquisitor, who had himself fed upon roots in the wilderness, suffered the tortures of damnation while trying to conquer flesh, in order to become free and perfect, but who had never ceased to love humanity, and who one day prophetically beheld the truth; who saw as plain as he could see that the bulk of humanity could never be happy under the old system, that it was not for them that the great Idealist had come and died and dreamt of His Universal Harmony. Having realized that truth, he returned into the world and joined—intelligent and practical people. Is this so impossible?"

"Joined whom? What intelligent and practical people?" exclaimed Alyosha quite excited. "Why should they be more intelligent than other men, and what secrets and mysteries can they have? They have neither. Atheism and infidelity is all the secret they have. Your Inquisitor does not believe in God, and that is all the Mystery there is in it!"

"It may be so. You have guessed rightly there. And it is so, and that is his whole secret; but is this not the acutest sufferings for such a man as he, who killed all his young life in asceticism in the desert, and yet could not cure himself of his love towards his fellowmen? Toward the end of his life he becomes convinced that it is only by following the advice of the great and terrible spirit that the fate of these millions of weak rebels, these 'half-finished samples of humanity created in mockery' can be made tolerable. And once convinced of it, he sees as clearly that to achieve that object, one must follow blindly the guidance of the wise spirit, the fearful spirit of death and destruction, hence accept a system of lies and deception and lead humanity consciously this time toward death and destruction, and moreover, be deceiving them all the while in order to prevent them from realizing where they are being led, and so force the miserable blind men to feel happy, at least while here on earth. And note this: a wholesale deception in the name of Him, in whose ideal the old man had so passionately, so fervently, believed during nearly his whole life! Is this no suffering? And were such a solitary exception found amidst, and at the head of, that army 'that thirsts for power but for the sake of the mean pleasures of life,' think you one such man would not suffice to bring on a tragedy? Moreover, one single man like my Inquisitor as a principal leader, would prove sufficient to discover the real guiding idea of the Romish system with all its armies of Jesuits, the greatest and chiefest conviction that the solitary type described in my poem has at no time ever disappeared from among the chief leaders of that movement. Who knows but that terrible old man, loving humanity so stubbornly and in such an original way, exists even in our days in the shape of a whole host of such solitary exceptions, whose existence is not due to mere chance, but to a well-defined association born of mutual consent, to a secret league, organized several centuries back, in order to guard the Mystery from the indiscreet eyes of the miserable and weak people, and only in view of their own happiness? And so it is; it cannot be otherwise. I suspect that even Masons have some such Mystery underlying the basis of their organization, and that it is just the reason why the Roman Catholic clergy hate them so, dreading to find in them rivals, competition, the dismemberment of the unity of the idea, for the realization of which one flock and one Shepherd are needed. However, in defending my idea, I look like an author whose production is unable to stand criticism. Enough of this."

"You are, perhaps, a Mason yourself!" exclaimed Alyosha. "You do not believe in God," he added, with a note of profound sadness in his voice. But suddenly remarking that his brother was looking at him with mockery, "How do you mean then to bring your poem to a close?" he unexpectedly enquired, casting his eyes downward, "or does it break off here?"

"My intention is to end it with the following scene: Having disburdened his heart, the Inquisitor waits for some time to hear his prisoner speak in His turn. His silence weighs upon him. He has seen that his captive has been attentively listening to him all the time, with His eyes fixed penetratingly and softly on the face of his jailer, and evidently bent upon not replying to him. The old man longs to hear His voice, to hear Him reply; better words of bitterness and scorn than His silence. Suddenly He rises; slowly and silently approaching the Inquisitor, He bends towards him and softly kisses the bloodless, four-score and-ten-year-old lips. That is all the answer. The Grand Inquisitor shudders. There is a convulsive twitch at the corner of his mouth. He goes to the door, opens it, and addressing Him, 'Go,' he says, 'go, and return no more... do not come again... never, never!' and—lets Him out into the dark night. The prisoner vanishes."

"And the old man?"

"The kiss burns his heart, but the old man remains firm in his own ideas and unbelief."

"And you, together with him? You too!" despairingly exclaimed Alyosha, while Ivan burst into a still louder fit of laughter.

Made in the USA
Lexington, KY
01 September 2019